God's Now Faith

Roger Coons

GOD'S NOW FAITH

Are You Looking for Answers?

For healing, safety, prosperity?

The are answers for life's challenges. *God's Now Faith* is a place to begin. May the words in this book change your life with new possibilities!

Introduction

A way to walk with the Lord and listen to His voice.

God's Now Faith is waiting for you to walk in it and be healed, delivered, set free from things that do not need to be there.

Just imagine being able to walk in the ways that Jesus did while here on earth, being able do what he did by walking in His faith. Being able to see and experience yourself and others receiving the good things that our Father in heaven has for us.

Acknowledgements

I would like to thank my wife Shirley Coons for the times she gave me the encouraging words to continue to work on this book.

I also would like to thank My Pastor Daniel Krawchuck for his encouragement and insights to make this book a success.

I would also like to thank my spiritual daughter Layla Rule for her contributions in the process of publishing my work.

Contents

God's Now Faith

By Roger Coons

1

God's Now Faith

Let us look at God's definition of faith.

Hebrews 11:1 "Now faith is a substance of things hoped for, the evidence of things not seen." NKJV

"Now faith is a confidence in what we hope for and the assurance about what we do not see." NIV

Let us start with **now**. It is not yesterday, two weeks ago, or a month or a year ago, it is **now**. It also is not tomorrow, because that is not here yet. As far as yesterday or in the past, that is all done with. **Now** is the best time, that starts in the meaning of faith. The scripture that **God's now faith,** making it clear we are to experience it in this moment.

It appears in the Bible. "But that without faith it is impossible to please Him, for he who comes to God must believe that He is, and that He is a rewarder of those who diligently seek Him." Hebrews 11:6 NKJV

We can trust in God and operate in His faith, knowing that He desires for us to succeed and be faithful with what He gives us. We can

1

then help others with the things and opportunities He gives us. It is especially important also that we really know that our Father loves us.

1 John 4:7. "Beloved, let us love one another, for love is of God; and everyone who loves is born of God and knows God." NKJV

John 15:10 "If you keep My commandments, you will abide in My Love, just as I have kept My Father's commandments and abide in His Love. 11. These things I have spoken to you, that My joy may remain in you, and that your joy may be full." NKJV

We can let His love flow in us and allow His joy to be full in us. If we are going to love others, we must love ourselves first. This will help us to operate in **God's now faith**. Our God operates in His Wonderful Love. We can allow His Love to direct our thoughts and ways.

Now operating in the faith that the Father gives us allows us to go forth and be successful.

Our purpose on this earth is to represent Him in His Kingdom and allow Him to work through us to help others and bring them to a knowledge of the living God. One of the hardest things to understand is to trust when you cannot see our Father in Heaven, but you can hear from Him.

When we ask God for something we will need to believe he hears and will answer us. Believing that now is the opportune time for our faith to be released and the answers to come. Too many times, we do not hold on to that **God's now faith**. The things that hinder our faith are unbelief and not trusting in the most faithful, our God. Our faith needs to stand on the fact that our God can be trusted for all that we ask of Him. He knows what we need before we ask Him. When we ask of Him, we need to believe that He hears and responds to what we ask. A loving Father wants to take care of his children. We need to know that our God is that loving Father and believe that He hears us.

> "My sheep hear My voice, and I know them, and they follow Me." John 10:27 NKJV

Since **faith** is **now**, we should believe that our Father hears us now. Trusting and believing are strong words, that need our attention and action. There are several scriptures in the Bible that we will talk about and discuss, they have to do with us believing what the Father is saying.

It is extremely important that we know what **now** really means, it does not mean past or future it means right this moment. It is better to learn to live in the present and walk in it.

We need to have that childlike faith. When we promise our children that we are going to do something or take them somewhere they believe us. It is only when we have promised our children and then break our promises that they act like they do.

Many times, we have asked God for things and if we do not get it, we become discouraged. Could that be when we are asking and not believing that we do not receive? Even if the answer is no, it is an answer. How much better it would be if we remember the many things that He has done for us through our asking?

What if the woman with the issue of blood thought in her mind, "If only I could touch the hem of His garment and tomorrow or next week I will be healed?"

Her faith was a **now** kind of **faith** that when she touched the hem of His garment she would be healed! That is the **God's now faith** that our Father wants us to operate in. Jesus walked in that kind of faith believing when He did what the Father wanted Him to do, it would be done.

When we pray asking Him to do something we must believe He has heard us and is able do what we are petitioning Him for.

When we walk away believing we have received and not doubting, it can happen. The best way to honor Him, is to thank Him for answering.

To have faith we will have to ask God and believe and then receive. We will need to live and walk in faith to see it grow. The coming days will require us to walk in faith, and it is by faith that you will hear the Lord speaking. It is your faith that will guide, protect, and provide for you.

We will talk more about the need to operate in His faith so that the provisions that you will need can come to you.

> Romans 5:1-2 "Therefore, having been justified by faith, we have peace with God through our Lord Jesus Christ, through whom we also have access by faith into this grace in which we stand, and rejoice in hope of the glory." NKJV

There are many places in the New Testament that give us practical ways to operate in the faith, that we will need as the days go on.

Once we recognize that our Father wants us to live in **God's Now Faith** all the time. We will be able to be healed and set free so we can help others.

2

Ask Believe Receive

Ask Believe and Receive

It is important to ask to receive. Along with that, we can believe then receive.

Let us go to Matthew 7:7 "Ask and it will be given to you; seek and you will find; knock and the door will be opened to you. For everyone who asks receives; the one who seeks finds; and to the one who knocks, the door will be opened. NIV

John 15:7,8. "If you remain in Me and My words remain in you, ask whatever you wish, and it will be done for you. This is to my father's glory, showing yourselves to be my disciples". NIV

John 16:23,24. "In that day you will no longer ask me anything. Very truly I tell you, My Father will give you whatever you ask in My name. Until now you have not asked for anything in My name. Ask and you will receive, and your joy will be complete". NIV

These are just a few of the scriptures that show you what happens when you ask. I believe that because we ask in faith, this will be the results of our asking, we will receive.

It is extremely important that we ask and believe that He has heard us and will answer.

We have already talked about our God listening to us. He desires to have a relationship with us and that will require speaking and listening. The fact that we believe that He hears us is extremely important. It would be terrible if when we talked to our friends or relatives and we did not believe they heard us. We walk in many paths of belief. We have faith that when we touch the light switch the light will go on. There are so many times that we operate in faith, however this faith we are talking about is when we are talking to God. When we talk to Him, we must believe that He hears and responds to us as His children.

This chapter is about asking, believing, and receiving.

So now that we have asked and believe God has heard, the next step is to receive. We can receive when we have asked and believed through this simple process. Many times, this process must circumvent our mind and go directly to our heart. Too often we are trying to manipulate things in our mind. Endeavoring to make those requests occur with our help, is sometime necessary.

Let us take the story of blind Bartimaeus, He was along the road crying out to Jesus.

"Many rebuked him and told him to be quiet, but he shouted all the more, "son of David, have mercy on me!" 49. Jesus stopped and said, "Call him." So, they called to the blind man, "Cheer up! On your feet he is calling you." 50. Throwing his cloak aside, he jumped to his feet and came to Jesus.
51. "What do you want me to do for you?" Jesus asked him. The blind man said, "Rabbi, I want to see."

52. "Go," said Jesus, "Your faith has healed you". Mark 10:48-52 NIV

Immediately he received his sight and followed Jesus along the road. This is an example of asking, believing, and receiving:

The blind man was bold enough to cry out to Jesus so that he would hear him then he asked and believed Jesus said, "Go your faith has healed you." This is a notable example of asking, believing, and receiving.

Another example of this type of healing is one of the rulers of the synagogue a man named Jairus.

Mark 5:22. "And behold one of the rulers of the synagogue came Jairus by name. And when he saw him, he fell at his feet and begged him earnestly, saying", "My little daughter lies at a point of death. Come and lay your hands on her, that she may be healed, and she will live." 24. So, Jesus went with him, and a great multitude followed him and thronged him.

35. While he was speaking, some came from the ruler of the synagogue's house who said, your daughter is dead. Why trouble the teacher any further?" As soon as Jesus heard the word that was spoken, He said to the ruler of the synagogue, "Do not be afraid; only believe." 37. and He permitted no one to follow Him except Peter, James, and John the brother of James.

38. Then he came to the House of the ruler of the synagogue, and saw a tumult and those who wept and wailed loudly. 39. When he came in, he said to them, "Why make this commotion and weep? The child is not dead, but sleeping." 40. And they ridiculed him. But when He had put them all outside, He took the father and the mother of the

child, and those who were with Him, and entered where the child was lying. 41. Then He took the child by hand and said to her, "Talitha, Cumi," Which is translated, "little girl, I say to you, arise." 42. Immediately the girl rose and walked for she was 12 years of age. And they were overcome with great amazement. Mark 5:22-42 NKJV

This is another place that the father of the child asked and believed and then received. So, you can see that first we must **ask**, then **believe** that He heard us and then this will allow us to **receive**.

Another example is the woman that touched His hem of a garment:

"And a woman was there who had been subject to bleeding for 12 years. 26. She had suffered a great deal under the care of many doctors and then spent all she had, yet instead of getting better she grew worse. 27. When she heard about Jesus, she came up behind him in the crowd and touched his cloak, 28. because she thought", "If I just touch His clothes, I will be healed." 29. "immediately her bleeding stopped, and she felt in her body that she was freed from her suffering". 30. At once Jesus realized that power had gone out from him. He turned around in the crowd and asked, "who touched My clothes?" 31. "You see the people crowding against you," his disciples answered," and yet you can ask, 'Who touched me?" 32. But Jesus kept looking around to see who had done it. 33. Then the woman, knowing what had happened to her, came and fell at his feet and, trembling with fear told him the whole truth. 34. He said to her, "Daughter, your faith has healed you. Go in peace and be freed from your suffering." Mark 5:25-34 NIV

This amazing testimony of her believing and receiving surely can stir up the reason to ask and believe so you can receive.

Our healings have been paid for. 1 Peter 2:24 NKJV. Who Himself bore our sins in His own body on the tree, that we, having died to sin, might live for righteousness--- by whose stripes you were healed.

Now we need to believe that we are healed now with the **God's now faith**. The power of the healing is believing and receiving.

When we allow our minds to accept what God has done for us though Jesus on the cross, then we can also receive.

In this world today we will need to walk and live in His **now faith**. He has made it possible for us to be in health.

3 John 1. "Dear friend, I pray that you may enjoy good health and that all may go well with you, even as your soul is getting along well". NIV

3 John 1. "Beloved, I pray that you may prosper in all things and be in health, just as your soul prospers". NKJV

Health and prospering are important to God. We can live in all He has for us, or we can stay in lack of health or prospering. These are times when we will want to walk in His ways to be able to help others with their needs.

3

Jesus Taught Needed Lessons

J esus taught needed lessons.

One day Jesus cursed a fig tree.

Matthew 21:18."Early in the morning, as Jesus was on his way back to the city, He was hungry. 19. Seeing a fig tree by the road, He went up to it but found nothing on it except leaves. Then He said to it, "may you never bear fruit again!" immediately the tree withered. 20. When the disciples saw this, they were amazed. "How did the fig tree wither so quickly?" They asked. 21. Jesus replied, "Truly I tell you, if you have faith and do not doubt, not only can you do what was done to the fig tree, but you also can say to this mountain, throw yourself into the sea and it will be done. 22. If you believe, you will receive whatever you ask for in prayer." Matthew 21:18-22 NIV

Jesus was teaching his disciples about authority and if they had learned the lesson when the sea was boisterous, they could have calmed it. He was trying to teach them that they could do things like He did. Let us look at that scripture that tells us about the storm with the disciples that were in the boat with Jesus.

Jesus calms the storm.

Starting in Matthew 8:23. "Then He got into the boat and the disciples followed him. 24. Suddenly a furious storm came up on the lake, so that the waves swept over the boat. But Jesus was sleeping. 25. The disciples went and woke him, saying, "Lord, save us! we're going to drown!" 26. He replied, "you of little faith, why are you so afraid?" Then He got up and rebuked the winds and the waves, and it was completely calm. 27. The men were amazed and asked, "what kind of man is this? Even the winds and waves obey him!" Matthew 8:23-27 NIV

I have been able to take authority over several storms. One day my family and I were are at a lake on the east side about to eat our supper. When I saw on the other side of the lake a huge storm was coming towards us. At that moment, I took authority and told that storm you stay there until we are done eating do not move in Jesus' name.

We were able to have our supper and pack up our things and get into the car and then the storm came across the lake, and it was a huge rainstorm.

Another time... I was at my son's wedding reception in their backyard. Thunder and lightning was intense around us, and I commanded that storm not come near us until we had finished our reception. We were able to enjoy the festivities, and it did not rain until the party was finished.

I believe that Jesus was teaching his disciples how to walk in the authority that they were going to have and operate in during their time on the earth.

When we walk in the **God's now faith** that God has given us, we could have authority over things He shows us. As time goes on and things on the earth and around the earth becoming increasingly troubling, we will be able to take care of the storms that come our way.

Much of what Jesus taught us in the scriptures will help us as we continue our journey here on earth.

Learning to take advantage of what Jesus did while He walked the earth will help us increasingly in the days to come.

4

Substance

S ubstance.

Hebrews 11:1. "Now faith is the substance of things hoped for, the evidence of things not seen". NKJV

Substance is the basis of something or the confidence. The reality is that substance is the confidence in things hoped for.

Whether we use confidence of reality, substance is something that's real. We can believe that when we ask God in faith, He hears us. As a result of that when we operate in **God's now faith**, we can be confident that answers are on the way, or we already have them.

Hebrews 11:1."Now faith is confidence in what we hope for and assurance about what we do not see". NIV

So, whether we read this verse in New King James Version or New International Version, there is something about the words used to describe primarily what faith is. We only must trust that our Heavenly Father has the answers. When we ask in assurance or confidence and believe that He has heard us, then something is about to happen.

My trust in God is that He is more interested in us receiving answers or healing than we can imagine.

Even though we have not seen or cannot see the things that are coming, it is important to ask God yo help us, we still must believe when those things are coming we can walk in **God's now faith**.

Can you imagine how much our Heavenly Father wants us to participate with him for the things that need to be done on this earth **now**?

This could be your day to ask, believe, and trust God and then receive the answers. Even though the substance or the confidence may not seem real to you, it is.

If we trust for our salvation how more is it to trust for our healing or those things we are asking God in faith for?

Is there something that you wanted from God and have not asked in faith for? Today may be the day that you could bring your request to a faithful God. Then, let Him take care of what you need. There is no time like **now** to let our request be made known to God.

5

Hope for

Hope For.

Hebrews 11:1. "Now faith is confidence in what we hope for". NIV

"Now faith is the substance of things hoped for". Hebrews 11:1 NKJV

The practical things that we hope for is wanting something to happen or receiving something. We all have hoped for something and by believing it is going to happen or come to us, it becomes the assurance when it happens.

I believe that God wants us to operate in this type of faith that requires hope also. I believe that many times we have hoped that something is going to happen and many times it does.

To walk in this **God's now faith** it will take *hoping* too. Nothing wrong with allowing our hearts to have healthy desires. It is when we stop hoping and resign ourselves to not believing that our God want us to be healed, healthy and prosperous that things start to fall apart. Now is the time to allow your hopes to become real and fulfilled. You hold the answer in your voice and belief.

6

Evidence of Things Not Seen

E vidence of things not seen.

Can you imagine having the evidence of things not seen?

"Now faith is the substance of things hoped for, the evidence of things not seen". Hebrews 11:1 NKJV

Evidence meaning is proof or confirmation. It could also mean affirmation, authentication, or substantiation. So, let us take proof to start with. When we want proof, we can go to our God and He can tell us what truth is in these situations. So, looking at what faith is has brought us to the facts and the evidence of believing that we can walk and live in His faith. This is going to be vital to God's Kingdom people as time goes on. We are only scratching the surface of those things that we will need to be able to walk out the life that He wants for us.

Now faith is vital for Kingdom people to be able to do business, buy and sell. Perhaps we will need to live in more of **God's now faith** to live and be able to worship together in our congregation.

Time is here that knowledge has increased, we may not be able to send our children to colleges. The places of higher learning may not be able to change their books and information fast enough.

Can you image that schoolbooks that will not be able to hold all the information that one would need to complete their education? Because of the constant changes in technology and information.

This will bring us into a new place of learning and walking in the **God's now faith** that will be needed. We will be able to do what God has called us to do. When we stay in the **God's now faith** that He has shown us, the things needed will happen. We will have to be patient and listen to what He has to say about even our learning. Since He has all knowledge and the information we will need, it would be vital that we listen to Him.

The practical application will be our having the ability and knowledge of where to look and find the information we will need.

7

Now and Future need For Faith

Now and the future need for faith.

What if we will need the faith to multiply food?

Have you ever wondered why Jesus' feed 5,000 and then repeated the feeding to 4,000?

Did Jesus show us this, so that we would be able to do it in the future? Is this event relevant for today?

I do not believe that story about feeding the 5000 was just a nice story. There is more to the story about Jesus and the disciples feeding the 5000 and the 4000. Remember, it was the food in the disciple's hands that fed the people. It was Jesus's faith that started the feeding. Events in the Bible are for us to realize that they could be used for today. I have seen food multiplied as we ate what we had poured from the pot.

Are we willing to take these truths and apply them for today?

Are we going to be able to help others to have the necessities of life by His faith? It is a wonderful thing for us to believe; however, we need to pass this on to others so they can do the same.

There are many places in the New Testament that give us practical ways to operate in the faith that we will need as the days go on.

How are we going to teach and or demonstrate, the need for them to operate in this faith?

What will it take to show others how to operate in this faith? How did Jesus attain the faith that He walked in?

Lots of questions, and there are lots of answers. We need to walk in the ways of this kind of **God's Now faith,** while bringing the Kingdom of God into the reality of this day and age. It is by faith that you will hear Him. Your faith will lead; guide, protect and provide for you.

We need to walk in the ways of this kind of **God's now faith**, while bringing the Kingdom of God into the reality of this day and age.

It is very interesting how Jesus reacted to storms. He in that moment took authority over them and commanded them to cease. That was a **now** kind of **faith,** He was operating in. There are times when storms try to come on our land, and we have authority over them. It will take the **God's now faith** to cause the storm to stop.

"Therefore, having been justified by faith, we have peace with God through our Lord Jesus Christ, through whom we also have access by faith into this grace in which we stand, and rejoice in hope of the glory". Romans 5:1-2 NKJV

The storm that Jesus calmed in the sea is another example of what we will need to do. We have authority over storms, and we will be able to walk in **God's now faith** to calm them.

Our faith is going to be tested, and we will have the opportunity to use the **God's now faith** in many circumstances. We are blessed and challenged to be living in this time. It will take us to be praying and asking the Father for many things that we will need, to walk in His ways and truth. He has called us for such a time as this. We will have to be united with those around us that think and operate in **God's Now Faith** and have this authority. It will take the now faith to help them to stop the things around them that are not good.

Have faith. Work in **God's now faith**. Live and walk in faith, and it will grow. The days ahead of you will need this **God's now faith**.

As we grow in His Faith, we will be able to help others too.

Let your Father teach you how to walk in His type of **God's now faith**. Start by asking Father to help you with something that you need or want to do.

Remember our God has so much more that we can imagine in His resources. He owns the cattle on the hill, and He owns the hill. Think big and be bold with your **God's now faith**.

Encouragement

This book was designed to give those that want to have a new way of living without the encumbrances that continue to want to take over over in our lives.

God's now Faith is a place in our lives where we can have success over the things that try to rule our lives with evil, sickness, depression, discouragement, and those that do not have the victory that they need.

Your time is NOW to walk and live in the place that was designed by God for you.

About the Author

Roger Coons: Husband. Father of six children. Many grandchildren. And, 4 great-grand children at present.

Spiritual father to countless spiritual sons and daughters around the US & Canada that Roger and his wife Shirley have shepherd. Originally from Rochester, NY. Roger currently resides in Myrtle Beach, SC with his wife Shirley Coons and their beloved dog, Princess.

Roger Coons

References

Scriptures taken from The Holy Bible, New King James Version. Copyright 1982 by Thomas Nelson, Inc.

The New King James Bible, New Testament Copyright 1979 by Thomas Nelson, Inc.

The Holy Bibles, New International Version

NIV Copyright 1973, 1978, 1984, 2011 by Biblica, Inc. Used by Permission. All rights reserved worldwide.

Holy Bible: New International Version

Published by Zondervan Grand Rapids, Michigan, USA

www.ingramcontent.com/pod-product-compliance
Lightning Source LLC
Chambersburg PA
CBHW051651120626
46551CB00015B/2309